SIMPLE

A Simple, Natural Approach to Discussing Sex With Your Children

TRUTHS

with Mary Flo Ridley

TABLE OF CONTENTS

This symbol indicates that the information that follows applies to the specified segment on the Step-by-Step DVD.

MAKE IT YOURS!

Simple Truths provides practical guidance, as well as personal opportunities, to modify the message and integrate your family's core values. Take advantage of the opportunities inside to reflect and write in this booklet. Feel free to highlight, underline, circle and mark up this booklet—whatever will help you retain and refine the information to make it work for your family!

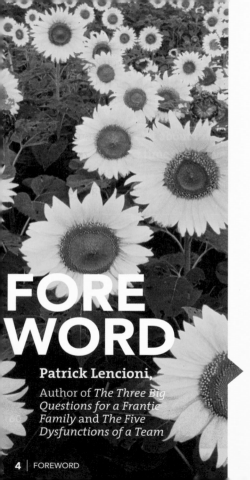

FORE WORD

Patrick Lencioni,
Author of *The Three Big Questions for a Frantic Family* and *The Five Dysfunctions of a Team*

The tragedy of marketing is that every company seems to present every product they sell as a must-have solution; something that will change a customer's life forever. This doesn't seem like much of a problem because we all learn to adjust our expectations and see the advertisements for what they are. However, the real cost of this modern over-marketing culture becomes particularly clear when we really do find a product that really will change a customer's life forever, and we're afraid no one will believe us. Call it the "marketeer who cried wolf" syndrome.

I explain all this so you'll believe me when I say that "Simple Truths" with Mary Flo Ridley will change your life. Well, that's not exactly true. More accurately, it will merely make your life less stressful. The life it will change forever is that of your child.

As a parent of four children, I worry about a lot of things. That's part of

> **And then we heard Mary Flo deliver the material you are holding in your hands, and our lives as parents changed forever.**

the job, I realize. However, one of the worries that seems particularly daunting is the one about how to help my kids have healthy attitudes and behaviors about sex.

So often when we look back at our own lives, we are amazed that we somehow navigated puberty, high school, college and single adulthood, and then managed to get married

of sending our own children out into the world to navigate those same rough waters without a guide. But we were paralyzed by what that guide should be.

And then we heard Mary Flo deliver the material you are holding in your hands, and our lives as parents changed forever. We immediately set aside any reticence or anxiety that we had about broaching the topic of sexuality. And though we are still knee deep in parenthood and nowhere near the end of shaping our children's sexual characters, the results have been stark already.

and have a family, all without really understanding the full magnitude and wonder and danger of this thing called sexuality. Of the many graces of God in my life, this is certainly one of the more appreciated ones.

It is no surprise, then, that my wife and I were mortified by the thought

Two of our boys had their fifth grade sex ed talk at school this year, and they weren't embarrassed, shocked or overly silly about it. When they hear a word or a phrase on the playground at school – and they hear plenty – they come to us with questions first. They know that sex is a wonderful gift that God gives them, but that is reserved for their spouse, and not to be used like a piece of athletic equipment or a means of social stature.

And perhaps most immediately gratifying of all, my wife and I are actually confident that they'll be able to deal with issues like pornography and peer pressure, as long as we continue to practice what Mary Flo teaches.

As is true of most of the groundbreaking concepts in the world, the messages here are as seemingly obvious as they are compelling. And that is what makes this all so powerful. Mary Flo distills what we need to know into a manageable, digestible collection of practical wisdom. Every parent will cling to this and recommend it to every parent they know. Really.

_____

Patrick Lencioni is founder and president of The Table Group, Inc., a specialized management-consulting firm focused on organizational health. He is the author of The Three Big Questions for a Frantic Family, The Five Dysfunctions of a Team, *and seven other best-selling books, and his work has been featured in Fast Company, Inc. Magazine, USA Today, Fortune and Harvard Business Review. Pat and his wife, Laura, are the proud parents of four boys.*

Our neighbors have four very active children. James, Catherine, John Thomas and Ben can often be seen in the front and side yards playing baseball, touch football, lacrosse, roller-blade hockey, basketball and volleyball with their friends.

Their garage/playroom is full of costumes, art supplies and an extensive array of Legos and building blocks. The backyard houses a sand box, swing set and extra space for an occasional bouncing house. They also have four rabbits, several cats and Henny Penny, the beloved chicken.

parties at Easter, block parties on the Fourth of July, birthday parties, science experiments, state fair projects, dance recitals and plays…we're talking a year-round celebration. And it all takes place on a piece of property measuring 70' x 160'.

So what if someone told them they could have an additional 70 x 20 feet of space for their playground? Wouldn't that automatically mean an extra amount of fun? After all, the additional room would mean more friends could come over, and more is always better, right?

Not when that extra play space is the street. From the earliest age we teach children **not** to play in the

And that's just the fun they have outside their house. Surely they have all the makings of a dreamy childhood. That family takes full advantage of every square inch of their property. Every season there's something special taking place: gingerbread house decorating parties at Christmas, egg coloring street. Why? Because it's dangerous! Everyone agrees that the risks aren't worth whatever potential reward it may offer.

The boundaries to the street aren't clearly marked by flashing lights or orange cones. They're just there. And so is the impending danger, even when cars can't be seen. The dangers of the street remain, even when kids start to ride their bikes around, and once again when they

No one disagrees with the value of play area boundaries. After all, we want what's best for our

> ❝Our culture promotes the notion that teen sex is normal, harmless and exciting.❞

start driving (at which point they have to look out for children and bike riders!).

children. So how come that same logic doesn't seem to apply to sex? How is it that boundaries suddenly become something so repressive and negative? It's just not very sensible.

Why do we let our society tell children that they will somehow "miss out" if we don't let them play with sex before the time that you—the person that loves your child more than anyone else in this world—determine as best for their future health and happiness? Our culture promotes the notion that teen sex is normal, harmless and exciting. In truth, it's a lot like playing in the street—there are severe, life-altering risks associated with doing it, even when not readily apparent.

The good news is that there's a perfectly wonderful and exciting setting for sex that's waiting to be explored without risks for those who prepare for (and live according to) a committed, life-long healthy relationship. As parents, it's our job to ensure that our kids understand the appropriate boundaries so they can enjoy a happy, healthy adulthood. It's a journey—one that can enrich your relationship in ways you can't even imagine.

LETTER
FROM
MARY FLO

As a parent, you work hard to prepare your children for the future. You want them to enjoy long, healthy and happy lives. You strive to nurture them in a loving family. You carefully make tough decisions about doctors, schools, activities, entertainment and playmates. You enthusiastically introduce them to sports, art, science and literature.

You also recognize the importance of developing your children's character. Values like honesty, respect, kindness, responsibility, loyalty, perseverance and courage are very important and they warrant intentional efforts for growth.

You are in a unique position of influence to shape your kids' hearts and minds before the rest of the to your children about sex can be daunting. The good news that I have for you is this: it does not

Seize the opportunity while your children are young to start having conversations that will forever shape their sexual character.

world gets their chance to try, and it's clear that the things you instill in them early will have an impact on their thoughts and actions for the rest of their lives.

Despite this exciting opportunity to influence, however, many parents are gripped by fear when it comes to shaping one key part of their children's lives: their sexual values. I understand that talking

have to be so frightening...in fact it can be very simple. Hear this: The first conversations you have with your children about sex will be extremely simple. All that you need to get started are the basic facts of biology and your values. The other very exciting news is that if we start these conversations when your children are young, you have the opportunity to make a very powerful first impression.

The goal of this approach is to give parents the tools to make these early first impressions about sex...through simple explanations of human bodies, birth and conception.

Parents who wait until their children near adolescence to attempt to conquer this topic are usually overwhelmed by the complexities before them. Parents who start in the early years with simple facts can then build on those facts as the years go by and can more easily handle the complicated issues when the time comes.

I want to encourage you to consider a different approach—to ponder what might be a radical thought: *Seize the opportunity while your children are young to start having conversations that will forever shape their sexual character. If you don't, someone else will. And they can't possibly care about your children's health and safety as much as you do.*

So come along and discover a smart and strategic way to share "Simple Truths" for a lifetime of rewards and benefits.

—Mary Flo Ridley

INTRODUCTION

My journey and passion to help parents positively affect their children's sexual character began accidentally some 20 years ago. When my children were young, I was a volunteer with a community service organization. Having been a high school teacher prior to having my own children, this was a great opportunity to provide training to others. One year, the leaders of our group were passing out topics for the trainers to discuss and a certain dreaded assignment landed in my lap: they wanted me to teach them how to talk to their kids about sex! My immediate thought was, "I am the last person on the planet that should be doing this."

You see, I grew up in a household where the word "sex" was never spoken. I had a wonderful, loving family but *that subject* was off limits. In fact, it took me 10 years just to get up the nerve to tell my parents that I helped people talk about sex with their kids. The truth is, even as an adult, I just never felt comfortable saying that word in front of my parents.

Once I delved into the assignment, I immediately sought out the opinions of "the experts." What these "experts" recommended, however, did not sit well with me. They made a presumptive, major assumption that all adolescent children will be sexual active. In a sense, they were equating our young people to any other animal in the wild kingdom, claiming that young people are incapable of controlling their sexual urges.

If you talk with your children early, you will earn their trust—a priceless asset that will make the truly difficult conversations much easier to navigate in the future.

I felt they deserved a lot better than that. I wanted to pave a new path—one that would capitalize on my child's natural curiosity without overexposing her to information that wasn't developmentally appropriate.

That volunteer assignment was the beginning of a lifetime journey for my husband, Dave, and me. We felt our approach to talking with our children was revolutionary, one that gave us great hope despite sometimes feeling we were very alone on our journey.

As a result, their ultimate advice was to focus all teaching on condoms and sexually transmitted diseases (STDs).

I do believe that there is a time and place for these discussions, but as a mother of young children, I didn't want those topics to be my children's first impression about sexual intimacy. Quite frankly,

"Simple Truths" is an expanded version of the plan Dave and I developed within our own family. Over the past 20 years, many families across the nation have found this basic framework to be very helpful. Right up front I want to be very clear on something: **I want you to personalize this strategy.** You could say what we said, but it is much more meaningful and significant if you work through the hard issues for your specific family and make these conversations personal and special. My goal is for you to process our lessons and experiences, internalize them and ultimately customize a specific plan that takes into account your family's unique values and personalities. Doing so will make this a very valuable experience for your family.

MAKE IT YOURS! ━━━▶

Think back to when your parents gave you "The Talk" (if they did at all!).

→ Was it awkward?

→ Was it too late?

→ Did it shape your views about sex and sexuality?

→ Did it affect your behavior?

→ At the end of the day, did you feel equipped? Overwhelmed?

Embarrassed? Ashamed? Confused?

→ Perhaps most importantly of all, did talking about it draw you closer to your parents or make you want to distance yourself from them?

→ What was the tone about sex in your home?

→ How do you want your children to think back on your conversations with them about sex?

→ Did the media play a key role in shaping your attitudes and behaviors about sex and sexuality? If so, how?

STARTING EARLY

The primary question I get from people is: **Why should I talk to my child about sex at such an early age?**

I believe an important part of parenting is preparing children for the future and shaping their character. It's a pretty accepted expectation that good parents play a major role in the social, intellectual and emotional aspects of their children's development, but Dave and I wanted to also shape our children's sexual character.

This approach might be considered radical to some because most parents think sexuality is a topic of

conversation best reserved for the teen years. To me, that's like trying to teach a child who has never been in the water to swim after they've fallen headlong into the deep end of the pool. If you wait, you may be too late.

If you start when they are young, you will encounter far less resistance and have far less repair work to do correcting the false ideas and values they absorb from the media. Starting early allows you to have natural conversations that evolve in response to your child's natural curiosity. It allows you to instill a solid foundation and purposeful framework for them to build on when the sensual images and messages of the media begin hitting them from all sides.

When they're young, your approach can be simple. You can help your child realize that their sexuality is just another beautiful part of who they are becoming. If you integrate these conversations into everyday moments (rather than having "The Sex Talk"—an awkward, one-time presentation that can't possibly do an adequate job of equipping your children for success), you will find your children retain much more of what you want them to know and embrace, and it won't be nearly as difficult or embarrassing.

MAKE IT YOURS!

▸ Has your child ever asked you about body parts at bath time?

▸ Does your child naturally wonder why a woman's belly is so large (pregnant)?

▸ Despite your most protective efforts, what kind of messages are your kids exposed to on the TV? Billboards? Radio? Playground? Magazines around the house or grocery stores?

▸ Have you become numb to the messages on programs and movies supposedly geared for children of their age?

MAKE IT YOURS!

WHY NOW?

Another question I often receive is:
Why do I have to talk about this now?

First and foremost, if you are going to get much out of this resource, you'll need to change your mindset of talking about sex from "have

You can help your children see their sexuality as something very special—something of such great value that it's worth passionately preserving and protecting.

If you start this conversation with your child now, you will have many opportunities to expand the conversation in an age-appropriate

 Earlier is better! Take advantage of the limited window of time you have to talk about the important things of life—while they still want to hear from you.

to" to "want to." Think about the opportunity before you! You get to equip your children with the knowledge and values that will guide some of the most important decisions they will make in their entire lives.

manner as they grow and mature. You will have a foundation to build upon as the years go by. You'll be ahead of the curve, preparing your child for what lies ahead. You'll be having natural conversations with

your child about a sensitive subject at a time when they are eager to hear what you have to say and are readily prepared to accept it. By the time your kids become teenagers, they're developmentally predisposed to be more independent in their thinking and less accepting of your counsel. Like it or not, teenagers think it's "cool" to question their parents. That's nothing new. And that's why

discussing sex with your children should start when they're young and unfold in an age-appropriate manner as they mature.

MAKE IT YOURS!

» Are you reluctant to talk about sex and sexuality with your child?

» What is preventing you from embracing this conversation?

» How can you partner with your spouse to develop your child's sexual character?

CULTURAL VACCINATION

Another common question I hear from hesitant parents is: **Is it possible to protect my child from this toxic culture?**

If you're hesitant about delving into these discussions, consider how vaccinations have stemmed the tides of epidemics in our country. Vaccinating a child when they are young protects them from life-altering diseases in the future.

(Note: I recognize that vaccinations are somewhat controversial in pockets of our country, but the point of my illustration is applicable, regardless.)

When you have values-based discussions with your child on

If you start talking to your child early, you'll get to them before the media (or another person) does. You will be preparing them for when they're exposed to a confusing situation because they will be processing it through a filter you already instilled in them.

sexuality, you're vaccinating them from the dangerous and faulty messages that pervade our culture. You are the expert, administering doses of antibody-like information that will build up your child's resistance to our toxic, over sexualized culture.

TEAMING WITH YOUR SPOUSE

One barrier that can prevent parents from having the necessary conversations with their children is that the spouses are not in agreement about what to do. If this is your situation, I encourage you to sit down and talk with your spouse about your shared goals for your children, and how sharing "Simple Truths" does not have to be overwhelming. In all honesty, when we first started, my husband thought it might be too much information for such an early age, but after further reflection he recognized that talking to a 4-year-old in an age-appropriate manner about sensitive issues would probably be more productive than attempting to start the conversation with a 13-

---

MAKE IT YOURS!

▸ What might your child be exposed to at someone else's home? What about when they are out in public with someone other than yourself or your spouse?

▸ How do you respond when your child sees an inappropriate act, image or message? Do you ignore it and hope they are too young to notice it? If they see it and you don't respond, does that normalize it to them? How can they know what is appropriate if you don't point it out to them?

---

year-old. It's important that you both weigh the risks vs. rewards of starting early in light of the overall goals you share for your children. Working through this process together can actually draw spouses closer together, and closer to their children as well.

For many families, however, parenting in partnership isn't even an option. If you are a single parent,

I implore you not to be discouraged. You can still share your values with your child, while pointing out that their other parent may have some differing views. Simply remind the child that you love them so much that you want them to hear from your heart about the things that really matter.

MAKE IT YOURS!

- ›› Are you and your spouse on the same page? If not, what's the root of your differences?

- ›› Have you discussed how your values and goals relate to your child's sexual character?

- ›› If your child's other parent is not in the home, is your relationship strong enough to work through a plan together on how to approach this topic? If not, commit to doing your part to protect your child's future health and happiness.

ANTICIPATING QUESTIONS

The key to good conversation is being prepared. That means thinking about what you want your child to know (which we'll cover in Step One). It also means anticipating the questions your child might ask and having answers prepared in advance. You'll need to consider the messages that pervade our culture. You'll want to listen to the conversations they have with their friends. You'll want to always be welcoming when they come to you with questions. Remember, you don't have to know all of the answers. You just have to be willing to search out the answers you don't know when a tough question arises.

One thing that's very important, regardless of the question they ask, is how you immediately respond.

Don't wait until it's too late! Establish yourself as a loving, knowledgeable authority in their lives early in order to be seen as a safe and reliable source of information. If you have older children, don't think it's too late to try. Apologize to them for not having conversations earlier and spend time with them to find out what they do and don't know, and what you can add to ensure your values are part of what they know.

What will your child see in your eyes? Shock? Fear? Nervousness? Discomfort? How about a comforting smile? That's what they need to see if you're trying to keep defenses down and lines of communication open. The more you do something, the better you get at it, so look in the mirror, practice smiling and use the reassuring phrase, "I'm so glad you asked." This reaffirms to your child that they came to the right place (and also gives you a few extra moments to collect your thoughts!).

MAKE IT YOURS!

▸▸ Has your child ever asked you a question about sex that caught you off guard?

▸▸ How could being prepared in advance change the way you feel about addressing your child's questions about sex?

▸▸ What do you think your facial expression will be when your child asks you a question about sex? What if it's something more graphic or detailed than you were expecting?

▸▸ How do you want your child to feel about coming to you with their questions about sex?

▸▸ Would anticipating their questions and thinking through answers in advance help you be more calm and confident when they come to you?

MAKE IT YOURS!

RECOGNIZING THE BENEFITS

Having these conversations early will allow you to be seen as the loving authority in your child's life, which is extremely valuable when more difficult issues arise—and they *will* arise—as you will have a solid foundation to build more delicate conversations upon. When you establish trust between yourself and your child, you will be seen as a credible source for information, which can draw you even closer to each other. If you wait until they are teens, you will most likely have limited trust and credibility and you will be competing with many other sources, most of which will seem much "cooler" than you at the time.

MAKE IT YOURS!

» Do you have a child who isn't very inquisitive about sexual things? If so, how can you start a simple conversation with your child that is respectful, but also informative?

» What are some things in your natural surroundings that could serve as good catalysts for conversation?

» Could you start a conversation using phrases like, "Have you ever wondered how…" or "Have I ever shared with you that…"?

STEP 1:

DEFINE
YOUR
MESSAGE

The first step in shaping your child's sexual character is to determine what you want your children to understand about sex, along with how you want them to think and act with respect to sex. You may already know what you *don't* want them to know. It's likely that you monitor what they watch on TV, who they play with and what they see on the computer. These are good preventative measures aimed at shielding them from the culture's confusing and distorted messages. The problem is, they're merely defensive. They're only half of the equation. A winning game plan requires offense *and* defense. So the question is, "What is your offensive plan?"

Here's another way to think about it. When your child is discussing their philosophy about sex and relationships with friends at college, what do you hope they'll say? Remember that what you tell them in the formative years growing up in your home will have a significant impact on their thoughts and actions when they're older.

Consider this: **What is it that you really hope your children know about sex and their sexual character by growing up in your family?**

MAKE IT YOURS!

» How did your own family of origin shape your sexual character?

» Were you adequately informed about sex by your parents?

» Did you feel comfortable talking with them about sex?

» Do you want your children to have a different experience than yours? If so, what would you intentionally change?

EXAMINING YOUR BAGGAGE

Before talking with your child about sex, you'll need to examine your own attitudes and opinions on the subject. Your discussions with your child should paint a positive picture of sexuality. This may be difficult for you to do if your past is affecting your perspective.

For many, sex hasn't been the beautiful experience they know it should be. Dating violence, rape and sexual abuse can all transfer such an extremely negative association with sex that it can be difficult to cast a vision beyond your painful past. This can further heighten anxiety about talking with your child about sex.

While it may be difficult, it's very important that you shift the paradigm and recognize that these conversations are not about your past—they're about your child's future. One should not be allowed to get in the way of the other.

A friend of mine is fond of saying, "Your past experiences can either be stepping stones or stumbling blocks. You get to decide." If there's baggage in your past, don't hide from it. Use it as a motivator to help your child avoid the same painful experiences.

Perhaps your own sexual behavior as a teenager was not what you want for your teen. That doesn't make you a hypocrite or disqualify you from having the right to influence your

child's decisions. If you've made mistakes with your sexual past, you are in a unique position to share the reasons you regret those decisions and why you want something better for your child. These conversations do not need to be detailed and would not be appropriate until the pre-teen/teen years. It just requires a shift in thinking and a willingness to be authentic for the sake of your child's future.

Here are some questions that may help you think through how your past may affect the way you shape your child's sexual character:

- What is the purpose of sex?
- Is love a feeling or an action?
- What decisions did you make about your own sexual activity?
- Which ones do you regret? If you had a chance to do it over, what would you have done differently?
- How can you learn from your past and use it to change the present and future?
- What choices do you want them to make?
- What decisions would most likely lead them to a healthy future?
- What are your hopes for your child's adult sex life?

- How do you want your child to view their masculinity/femininity?
- How do I hope they will interact with the opposite sex?

While it may be easier said than done, making peace with your past is an integral part of creating a positive legacy for your child's future. Finding that peace may be a painful journey, but rest assured both you and your children will be better for it.

Here are a couple quick insights provided in that helpful resource for parents:

1. **Take an honest look at your life.** Healing will come after a genuine review of your life experiences and mistakes. This includes looking at how others have let you down and how the choices you made affected your life.

How and where does this type of healing begin? That's an important question that extends beyond the scope of this particular resource, so while I can't devote the space necessary to adequately cover that topic here, I recommend a book several friends of mine wrote a few years back called *Questions Kids Ask About Sex.*

2. **Talk with a trusted friend or a professional counselor.** Find a reliable person with whom you can share not only the

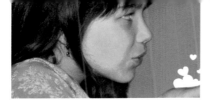

experiences described above, but also the feelings that came from your experiences. Healing is unlikely outside of relationships, and talking with a trustworthy friend or counselor can provide a tremendous sense of relief from the pain and sadness of your past.

3. **Grant forgiveness.** This is perhaps the most difficult part of the process. Forgiveness of those who have wronged you, and forgiveness of yourself for making mistakes in the past, are essential to free you to help your children develop a healthy sense of self-worth and their sexuality. Forgiveness isn't the same as forgetting—and it doesn't matter if the person has asked for forgiveness. It's truly a process of letting go and moving forward. Forgiveness is a gift you give yourself.

4. **Learn more.** It's never too late to become a student again. In the process of talking with your kids about sex and their sexuality, take the opportunity to glean new information from trustworthy sources so you can positively shape your children's future relationships.

MAKE IT YOURS!

DEVELOPING YOUR MESSAGE

We're ready to move into the essential building block assignment: **Work with your spouse to develop an over arching banner message regarding sex.**

This is where you must personalize it specifically to your family's values. It's perfectly acceptable, and perhaps even preferable, that your message differs from those of your friends or relatives. This is not a complicated series of points. It's a summary statement that serves as an anchor and compass for all other points of conversation to come. Decide what will work in *your* home.

Here are a few examples to help you better understand what I'm talking about:

The Ridley's Approach

When Dave and I went through this process, we wanted to incorporate our core beliefs and our closely held values. We wanted the framework of our children's conceptualization of sex to be something positive and something that placed sex within a specific context. What we came up with was that **"Sex is a gift from God for marriage."** This was the central message we wanted our children to know from growing up in our family.

A Health-Based Approach

A very good friend of mine is a school nurse and she's very concerned about how our children's sexual health will affect their futures. Her key message for her family was: **"Considering your future and your health, postpone sex until marriage."** Instead of using a faith-based approach such as ours, she fashioned her message based on their future health and success. Our messages differed somewhat, but that's simply a reflection of the different values of our individual homes.

A Fear-Based Approach

When I first starting doing this, I challenged my sister and her husband, who had two young girls at the time, to think about what they wanted their children to know about sex from growing up in their home. A few weeks later,

my brother-in-law enthusiastically shared that he was thrilled with their statement. I asked him what it was and he quickly replied, "Here's what I want my girls to know: **'Sex is like that electrical plug over there—you touch it, you die!'** After we laughed together, I asked him about their future, and wouldn't he want sex to be a wonderful part of their marriages? Mike wasn't budging. "I'll let their husbands come up with a different message... I like mine!"

You get the point. There are many different ways to approach developing your message. The key is that it be *your* message. That's what makes this exciting. It's all about your family's unique perspective.

MAKE IT YOURS! ✏️

- What are your core beliefs?

- What are your closely held values?

- What would you say is the purpose of sex?

- What do you wish you had known about sex from an early age?

- What do you hope for your child's sex life when they're older?

- How do you want your kids to remember your conversations with them about sexuality?

- What do you want your tone to be? Approachable? Fearful? Ashamed? Exciting?

- Do you desire that your child grasps the emotional complexities of sexual activity?

- Do you want your child to recognize the physical risks associated with having more than one sexual partner in their life?

- Do you hope your child saves sex for marriage? If not, when would you be comfortable with them being sexually active?

- Do you hope your child will establish clear boundaries and develop self-restraint in order to control the destiny of their sexual health?

INTEGRATING YOUR CORE VALUES

Talking through the list of questions below can help you identify both areas of agreement and conflict.

It will be much easier to develop your banner message when you define the common ground you share and talk about each of your own thoughts and experiences that shape your perspectives about sex.

- Are you pleased with the way your parents discussed sexual issues with you? If not, what do you want to do differently?

- How do you think today's cultural attitudes about virginity compare with those of 20 to 30 years ago? Are the pressures to be sexually active much different than when you were a teenager?

- What are the emotional and physical risks of sex outside of marriage?

- Under what conditions would you approve of your child having pre-marital or extra-marital sex?

- What role should sex play in marriage?

- How much influence do the following factors have on your sexual values:
  - Your parents
  - Your peers
  - Your family members
  - Your faith
  - The media
  - Educators
  - Medical professionals
  - Community leaders
  - Commentary from "Sex Experts"

- Which of these do you think will influence your children the most?

- What are the benefits of delaying sexual intercourse until marriage? What are the disadvantages?

- How would you feel and respond if your child were to either get

pregnant or impregnate someone? What would you expect them to do about it? What would you do as parents to try to avert that situation?

▸ Which of the following topics would be most difficult to discuss in your family:
  · Drugs and alcohol
  · Homosexuality
  · Masturbation
  · Pornography
  · Sexually transmitted diseases
  · Contraception
  · Teenage pregnancy
  · Prostitution
  · Abortion

▸ Would you rather be passive or proactive when it comes to protecting your child's health and future happiness?

▸ What are the greatest threats to your child's sexual health and values? How can you address those threats?

▸ What does it take to be an approachable, "askable" parent?

Your core message will be the overarching banner that provides direction and context to all conversations about sex and sexual activity.

MAKE IT YOURS!

- What are the facts and values you want to share with your child? What do you want them to know when?

Examples of Facts
- Proper names of body parts
- Factual story of conception (this may be revealed in progressive stages of depth and detail)
- True story of birth
- Reproduction is a natural part of all living things
- Concepts of modesty and privacy
- Concept of what's "appropriate" at various stages of development:
  - Where and when it's appropriate to be naked
  - With whom it's appropriate to talk about sexual issues
  - What types of affection

(touching, kissing, hugging) are appropriate for the various people in their lives
- Explanation of a mother's monthly cycle
- Physical and emotional changes that accompany puberty

Examples of Potential Values

‣ Our bodies are good
‣ We have a responsibility to care for our bodies
‣ Love is not just a feeling
‣ You can trust me to be a source of accurate information
‣ Any question you have is important to me
‣ Babies are valued from the moment of conception

‣ It is natural to be curious about our bodies
‣ Babies are a tremendous responsibility
‣ It is preferable to use correct names for body parts and functions
‣ Some things should always be private
‣ Nobody should pressure you to do something you don't want to do
‣ Your future is shaped by the choices you make today
‣ Past mistakes don't have to be repeated

Examples of Faith-Based Values

▸ You were created by God
▸ God made boys and girls different
▸ God's designed that it takes a Mommy and a Daddy to make a baby
▸ Sexual intercourse is a blessing from God for marriage
▸ God intends for our bodies and minds to mature over time
▸ God gives us boundaries to protect us
▸ God decided to make you a boy or a girl
▸ God made our bodies to feel good
▸ God calls us to have self-control

Which of these values do you and your spouse agree and disagree with?

What are some additional values you would add to your list?

MAKE IT YOURS!

_____
_____
_____
_____
_____
_____
_____
_____
_____
_____
_____
_____
_____
_____
_____
_____

PERSONAL VALUES ASSESSMENT SURVEY

This series of controversial statements* is designed to provoke discussion between you and your spouse as part of the process of defining what you want your children to know. **Feel free to strongly agree or disagree with these statements.** The point isn't to prove or disprove them, but rather for the both of you to express your feelings about them.

1. Sexual intercourse is a natural part of any meaningful relationship.
2. Men prefer to marry virgins.
3. Accurate knowledge about sex encourages sexual activity among young people.
4. Prevention of pregnancy is the female's responsibility.
5. It is better for males to have sexual experience before they marry.
6. Petting is a normal part of the teen experience.
7. Sex is a vital part of a healthy marriage relationship.
8. Marriage should be exclusively between a man and a woman.
9. Contraceptives should be available to teenagers without parental consent.
10. Pornography encourages sexual experimentation and can alter a person's satisfaction with their partner.
11. A family consists of any group of people who love each other (same sex or otherwise).
12. Masturbation is a normal, harmless release of sexual tension in adolescence.

*These statements are for discussion purposes only and do not necessarily reflect the author's personal views.

In the early years, the goal is to share the basics of biology and your family's core beliefs and values.

13. Sexual intercourse belongs only within the confines of marriage.
14. Knowledge of sexually transmitted diseases deters sexual activity.
15. Beauty makes men and women more valuable.
16. Sex is more exciting when you are young.
17. Sex is more exciting outside of marriage.
18. There is no such thing as safe sex.
19. It's unrealistic to think teenagers can exercise self-control.
20. Being a virgin is something to be ashamed of.

The dangers and pleasures associated with sexual intercourse are not appropriate to discuss when children are young. They will be introduced and discussed at a later date.

Establishing a clear, healthy message about sex lays the foundation for greater exploration of the mysteries and beauties surrounding sexual intimacy as your children mature. No matter how much you prepare your child, the culture will continue to have an influence on what your child knows and believes about sex. As parents, we need to find our own voice, and speak clearly and intentionally with it to counter the misleading and misguiding messages that surround our children. You are the most important person in your child's life. They need to hear about sex from someone who knows and loves them more than anyone else. They need to hear about it from you.

By this point, you're probably ready to take a breather. I'm guessing you didn't expect to have quite so much to consider in the process of developing your banner message. Don't be overwhelmed! Remember, your main goal at this point is to complete the following sentence: **What I want my children to think about sex as a result of growing up in my house is:** _____

_____

_____

_____

_____

_____

As a parent, you have to take
ownership of this issue. The more
excited you are, the more likely it
is you will recognize life's natural
teaching opportunities that surround
you and your children.

 **The perspective we want to offer our children is that
of a caring expert who is knowledgeable and eager
to share.**

**Once you've completed the foundational work
of defining your message, it's time to start the
conversation.**

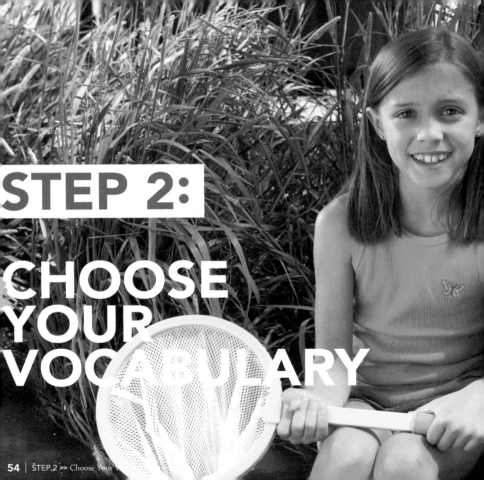

STEP 2:

CHOOSE YOUR VOCABULARY

DEVELOPING YOUR VOCABULARY

If you're going to talk with your children, you're going to need words. Sounds simple enough, but exactly which words should you use (and avoid for that matter)? When I started on this journey, I had no words. Or to be more specific, I had just one word. When it was bath time I would say, "Be sure to wash your earlobes and your knuckles and your ankles" and so on. Every body part had a regular name—except for those located in the area between the legs. For *those* particular parts of the body, I referred to them as "your privates." I even whispered the words "privates," as if it was were some special secret to keep.

very private! And now you know." That was all I could say if I had no other words to share with her.

If the first time your children hear you say "penis" and "vagina" is when you are explaining sexual intercourse, they will SO hear those words! The problem is, that may be about the only thing they do hear. It is important to start using the correct medical terminology at an early age. Doing this causes a couple of key things to happen. First, it makes you appear to be an authority on this subject. If you only use those "wingy-wangy" words (and we all know what those are), it's less respectful of their bodies. It also makes you look a little silly. Trying to give a serious explanation of conception

Once I was ready to start talking about sex with my child, I soon realized I was very limited in what I had to work with. With only one word to use, my explanation would have to sound something like this: "You see honey, Daddy has privates and mommy has privates and they get together and they...do something and birth to a captivated pre-teen using these cutesy, nondescript words diminishes your credibility significantly. If you start out using the proper medical terms for "their privates" rather than those "wingy-wangy" words, you will retain your authoritative stature and normalize the terminology so that it's not a distraction from the actual information you want them to understand. But why are we so reluctant to give them these words? Because they'll have them! And use them out loud (possibly in front of others like in-laws and neighbors!). So in addition to teaching them these words, you'll also need to talk to them about the appropriate times to talk about (and people to talk with) body parts.

Since those words weren't spoken in my family growing up, I was a little shy about using them, and even a little perplexed about how to start. So there I was mulling it over in my mind washing the dishes one morning when I overheard

Mr. Roger's singing a song on his children's program. I was listening to the words of his song when it suddenly clicked and I figured out how I was going to introduce these words to my children. The words to his song were, "Some are fancy on the inside, some are fancy on the outside, everybody's fancy, everybody's fine, your body's fancy and so is mine." Suddenly I knew how to start.

The Fancy Song Breakdown

Maybe you didn't catch it, so here's a closer look. "Some are fancy on the outside." That would be the male part of the body that's used to make babies. It's very fancy (or at least most men seem to think so!) and it's on the outside. The second line says, "Some are fancy on the inside." A female's baby-making equipment is on the inside. You can't really see it, so that's the fancy part of the female.

The second verse includes the phrase, "Only girls can be the mommies, only boys can be the daddies." So there was my opportunity. We sang the fancy song several times together before I got up the nerve to ask my child,

"Do you know what we are singing about?" "No." she replied. "We are singing about privates," I said. "No!" she exclaimed. "Yes, and they have fancy names that I'm now going to share with you." And that was how it began.

The more you say certain words, the easier it will be to use them in the future. If necessary, take some time to practice saying these words in the mirror—especially if you're uncomfortable.

You can really dazzle your children with the right medical terms for body parts. And that's great, because impressing them with your knowledge helps you claim your rightful place as the loving authority in their lives. It will serve you well to have your children thinking, "Wow! My parents are smart and know a lot about this." That way, the next time they have another question, they'll know just where to go for the answer!

MAKE IT YOURS!

- ▸ What words have you been using for your child's body parts?
- ▸ What words have you been using to describe body functions?
- ▸ What words were used in your family growing up?
- ▸ Can you see the value of using correct terminology?
- ▸ If you need to introduce the correct terminology, how might you initiate it?

MAKE IT YOURS!

DAZZLING DEFINITIONS

Let's be honest, it's been just a few years for all of us since we sat in a high school biology or health class. Don't be overwhelmed! You can explain basic male and female anatomy with these simple definitions:

Male Anatomy

Penis The "fancy" part between the legs of boys that allows them to pee and transfer sperm to a Mommy when it's time to make a baby.

Testicles A pair of round structures below a Daddy's penis that make and store sperm.

Sperm The seed that's deep inside a Daddy that meets with something deep inside a Mommy (egg) to make a baby. Use the seed analogy to explain the components of reproduction.

Anus The hole in a boys' or girls' bottom where undigested food comes out.

Female Anatomy

Vagina The place between a Mommy's legs where a baby comes out during normal birth.

Ovary A part inside a mommy that stores a mommy's eggs.

Egg The something that's deep inside a Mommy that meets with something deep inside a Daddy (sperm) to make a baby. Use the seed analogy to explain the components of reproduction.

Uterus The place inside a Mommy where a baby grows for about nine months until it's ready to live outside of the Mommy.

Birth Canal The pathway between the uterus and the vagina through which a baby travels during birth.

Contractions The tightening of the muscles around the uterus that sends the baby out of the uterus, through the birth canal and out the vagina (unless a C-section is required).

Umbilical Cord A part of the Mommy that is attached to a baby's tummy that allows for the baby to receive nutrition while living inside the Mommy. When the baby is born, the cord is snipped and tied, and the tied part becomes a baby's belly button.

Caesarean Section (or C-section) An alternative form of delivery for situations when the baby does not have a straight shot through the birth canal. When this occurs, a doctor usually senses the problem and makes a slit near where the baby is and lifts it out.

STEP 3:

EXPLAIN THE STORY OF BIRTH

 # THE STORY OF BIRTH

"Mommy, how does that baby get out of there?"

That is one of those phrases that strikes fear and panic in the hearts of parents everywhere. Perhaps the only one that inflicts more anxiety is the one that comes a little later: "Mommy, how did that baby get in there in the first place?" Fortunately for us, we usually only have to tackle one of them at a time. Children typically ask the "getting out" question first. Later, the "getting in" puzzle has to be solved. This is chronologically out of order, but it seems wiser to follow the developmental timeline of their questioning minds. Plus, it makes telling the stories a bit easier.

When your child asks the question (or if you feel it is a good time to initiate the conversation), it's important to be enthusiastic about discussing this topic. If you don't react with alarm, discomfort or embarrassment you will be able to keep the conversations concise and clear. Much like my friend's big black dog, children can smell fear and quickly grow uncomfortable if they sense uncertainty or inner turmoil in the person they're looking at.

Again, the key to overcoming fear is preparation. You know certain questions are coming, so practice giving the simple, factual answers beforehand. Here are some succinct, accurate answers for their common questions:

Q: *"So Daddy, how does the baby get out of Mommy's tummy?"*

A: Well sweetheart, I am so glad you asked because, actually, that baby is not in the mommy's tummy! It's in her uterus. By design [or by God's design], this is how a baby is born. It starts out very tiny in a mommy's **uterus**, and it grows and grows over about nine months of time. When the growing time is up, the baby sends the mom a signal. It's very clear. And this signal is the tightening of the muscles around the uterus, which is called a **contraction**. What it does is start sending the baby out of the uterus through the birth canal and out a special opening between the mommy's legs called the **vagina**.

When the baby comes out it's actually still connected to the mother with an **umbilical cord**, which is how the baby has been getting all of its nutrition. When the baby is delivered, the doctor will snip that umbilical cord and then we have our baby. Pretty amazing! And did you know your cute little belly button used to be your umbilical cord? Now sometimes a baby will be in the **uterus** and it will wiggle as it is going toward the **birth canal** it may not be a straight shot out. When a doctor senses this, the doctor makes a slit close to where the baby is and lifts the baby out of the mommy. That is called a **cesarean section**, or since it's such a big word, we often just call it a c-section. That is how your cousin,

Emma, was born, and that is why her head is so pretty!"

Be sure to let your child know that there are two ways that babies are born, because if they only hear about vaginal birth from you, and then hear their cousin was born via c-section, they are in for some very confusing exchanges around the table at Thanksgiving!

Here's an alternative approach to answering the same question.

Q: *"So Mommy, how are babies born?"*

A: "I'm so glad you asked, because that is a good thing for children to know. You are old enough now to learn about the wonderful way God designed this to happen. I know you think that a baby is inside a mommy's tummy, but it's not actually in the stomach, because that's where food goes after we swallow it. Instead, the baby is in a special place below her stomach called the uterus. That's the fancy name for the fancy part inside the woman where the baby grows. Every girl has a uterus. Boys don't have this special part because boys don't have babies. The baby starts out tiny and grows in the uterus for about nine months. At that point, the baby will have grown all the parts needed to live outside of this special place, and so it sends a signal to the mommy that it's ready to leave the womb. The muscles around the uterus then begin to push the baby out of the uterus through a little passageway called the birth canal, and out through a hole between the mommy's legs called a vagina. It's very exciting when this happens.

Have you ever seen your baby cousin wiggling in her crib? That's what a baby sometimes does when it can't travel straight down the birth canal. If it gets stuck, the doctor can tell what's happening and he will make an incision close to where the baby is and lift the baby out. This is called a Caesarean section or a c-section, and it can leave a mark that looks like a zipper."

The story of birth may become one of your favorite stories to tell because it is so amazing and beautiful. To be sure that you tell the story right, you should practice telling it over and over until you know you have the order of events down correctly. You're not a doctor and you don't have to be perfect, but the information you give should be accurate. This is a perfect opportunity to dazzle your child with your knowledge and vocabulary.

MAKE IT YOURS!

▸ Are you comfortable using the sample conversations above? If not, take a moment to write out the key phrases you'd like to communicate to your child.

_____

_____

_____

_____

_____

_____

_____

_____

_____

_____

_____

_____

_____

_____

STEP 4:

EXPLAIN REPRODUCTION

TEACHING OPPORTUNITIES

Now that you have told the story of birth, I want you to go back to nature and think about reproduction and the pattern and design of all living things. When my grandparents where growing up they didn't have to come to a class because they saw it all on the farm. They could see the cows dancing out in the meadow and then before too long there were baby calves. In major cities today, it's not like that. Everything is so urban there just isn't a lot of obvious nature to observe.

KEEPING IT NATURAL

If you're intentional about it, however, you can still use nature to explain the

what it takes to make another living thing just like it. Show your child how the seeds are deep inside the apple to protect them. Make a game of it, challenging your child to find the seeds of a strawberry, banana, cucumber, etc. Help them become a student of seeds, fascinated with eggs and captivated by the miracle of growth.

When our children were little, we used the phrase, "inside of every living thing is part of what it takes to make another living thing just like it." Note that I said "part" of what it takes. Reproduction doesn't take place in a vacuum. To make the point, place an apple seed on the counter and ask your child if that seed will grow into an apple all by itself. Even

wonder of reproduction. Simply take advantage of opportunities that are part of your normal, weekly routine. Make snack time learning time! Slice open an apple, but instead of dumping the core down the garbage disposal, show the inside and seeds to your child, pointing out how deep inside every living thing is a piece of preschoolers recognize that it takes good soil, water and sunshine for the apple to grow. Emphasize to your child that multiple things have to come together to create another living thing. This is a simple, natural concept that serves as a logical entry point for discussing answers to the impending question, "Mommy, how did the baby get in there?"

True Story

There once was a little girl entering her first day of kindergarten. She was disappointed that her best friend was not in her class, so her parents encouraged her to make new friends. Three weeks into the school year, the little girl came home and sat down to have a snack with her mother. "How was school today?" the mother asked.

The little girl replied, "It was good. I made a new friend, but I don't think you are going to let me play with her after school." The mother said, "Oh, really? Why not?" The little girl continued, "Well, after school her 16-year-old brother watches her until her mom gets home, and after school, she watches him have sex with his girlfriend."

The mother was shocked. I know, because I was that mother and this was my little girl telling me about her new friend. She was sitting on a stool, and as I was standing next to her I felt the blood suddenly go out of my legs and it suddenly became difficult to stand. In my racing mind I thought, *"You are right. I am not going to let you play with her after school!"*

I called the school and they handled it wonderfully. The counseling team started researching the story to find out what was really going on. They met with the family, and it turned out that, yes in fact, the 16-year-old-brother was having his girlfriend over when his parents were gone. And yes, they were going farther than they should, although they weren't going all the way. They were in his parent's bedroom and it was not a good situation. The situation was quickly and successfully remedied, with a new babysitter chosen.

Now that you aren't worried about our daughter's friend, you can focus back on me. Before I hit the floor, I said, "You are right, Jill, you are not going to get to play at her house." Then I asked,

"You are only five, how did you know this wasn't a good situation?" She responded, "Well, you said that sex is supposed to be for people who are married and they are not married. I asked!" She continued. "And Daddy said that sex is private and that no one should watch." When did he say that?, I wondered. Then I remembered when we would be watching TV and a commercial would come on where the actors would be rolling around in bed, Dave would change the channel and say, "I hope that they are married because that is really private, and no one should ever watch."

Wow. At just the third week of kindergarten, she was being exposed to sexual information. It was at that point that I knew Dave and I had chosen the right path for our family. If we hadn't gotten to her first, she probably would have asked her friend what sex was. As a result, her first explanation of sex would have been from a little girl whose older brother was sneaking his girlfriend into the house and messing around with her when he was supposed to be watching his little sister.

absorbs whatever information comes their way."

It became clear to both of us that, while the natural tendency might be to avoid talking with young children about sex, the reality is that it was much better to prepare our child for the times when we couldn't be there to shield them.

FILLING THE SPONGE

While I was cleaning up the kitchen that night, I told Dave about what happened that day. Holding the sponge I was using, I said, "You know, Dave, it's like there's a sponge in their minds. And that sponge is labeled, 'Curiosity about sexual things.' It just

Who Will Fill the Sponge?

When we originally considered having this conversation with our children, we were worried about exposing them to unnecessary and possibly age-inappropriate information. As we reflected on the two options—tell or don't tell—we concluded that age appropriate information was power. And we wanted our kids to be empowered. We felt that by arming our children with the basics wrapped in our values, our children would actually be more protected. Jill's story confirmed that for us.

Sponge Anatomy

What is a sponge? It's something that absorbs and retains whatever it comes in contact with. A sponge can actually absorb more when it is

filled slowly but consistently (drip by drip), rather than doused by a bucket of water.

Using sponge logic, the same concept applies to disseminating information about sex in small doses over a steady period of time. Dumping the bucket is like having "the talk." Drip, drip is like following the plan I've outlined in "Simple Truths." More retention through small, steady exposure.

Another interesting characteristic of sponges is that they don't absorb much if they're already full. My first inclination was to send my daughter off to school with a dry sponge. If I had done that, her first impression of sex would have been, "Well, I don't know what sex is, but I know it is for 16-year-olds and that other people watch." She would have soaked that right up. Instead, the information we poured into her prevented the wrong message about sex to sink in.

You have a clear choice to make. You can either fill your child's sponge, or let somebody else fill it— somebody who probably doesn't share your family's values and your commitment to their best interest.

PEER INFLUENCES

It's important to remember that with respect to filling the sponge, your family dynamics affect the urgency of getting there even earlier. That's because, culturally speaking, all of your children are the age of your oldest child. They're exposed to the media your oldest child views, hears and reads, and they're likely to

overhear at least some of the conversations that take place between your oldest child and his friends. To a large extent, this is unavoidable, so rather than relying on shielding your younger children, it's very important to prepare them. You can't always be around them to intervene.

Undoubtedly, peers will have a certain amount of influence over our children, and more so as their world enlarges beyond your home. Words and attitudes from older siblings and their friends will make their way into your child's vocabulary and attitudes; life just unfolds that way. The beauty of this plan: Parents can get there first, and often. First impressions are powerful, and the constancy of your message can make the difference.

The positive, health-filled messages and attitudes that you send your child (that drip, drip into their sponges on a regular basis) will be a deterrent to some of the wrong ideas and degrading words.

If we want our children to have a truthful look at what should be a beautiful part of their lives, we will have to get that message to them ourselves. We cannot rely upon other institutions to do the heavy lifting. Families are the perfect place for children to learn about all of this, and in the next chapter we'll tackle one of the most feared conversations.

MAKE IT YOURS!

STEP 5:

EXPLAIN
CONCEPTION

Welcome to the big time. There is no turning back. We've now reached the heart of the matter; the million dollar question: "How does a baby get in there?" Everyone wants to know how to answer this question. It's the reason you're reading this now, so keep reading for the answer.

THE STORY OF CONCEPTION

Once you know the answer, the immediate next question is, "When should I start? When my child is three? Four? Seven?"

At the risk of sounding evasive, there's no simple one-size-fits-all answer to the "When should I start?" question. Here's why. There are 6-year-olds... and then there are 6-year-olds. Their age is the same, but their situation is not. The first 6-year-old is a first born 6-year-old. He watches 6-year-old music, knows what is on his 16-year-old brother's iPod and what's under his 16-year-old brother's bed.

 A family is the age of their oldest child, and everyone else just has to keep up!

TV, tells 6-year-old jokes, and knows 6-year-old songs. And because he is a first-born, he has three healthy meals and a healthy snack each day, he gets regular reading time and actually takes a nap at naptime. Then there is the second 6-year-old, who is every bit as six, looks just the same, but this 6-year-old is the youngest of four. This 6-year-old has a 16-year-old brother. As a result, this 6-year-old lives in a 16-year-old world. He watches 16-year-old TV, listens to 16-year-old music, knows what is on his 16-year-old brother's iPod and what's under his 16-year-old brother's bed.

They are physically the same age, but they are not the same emotionally or experientially because they have not grown up in the same aged environment. So there really isn't a specific right age to begin talking about sex with your child. The question becomes less about "When do I talk to my child?", and more about, "Do I want to be the one to tell them?" If you wait much beyond kindergarten, you probably won't be the first one to talk about it with them.

> **If you are a parent of a preteen (ages 9-12) who hasn't asked any questions, and you haven't engaged them in a conversation, I highly encourage you to schedule a time as soon as possible to sit down and discuss your child's opinions, assumptions and questions about sex. Share your hopes and dreams for their sexual behavior.**

Do you really want to risk the wait? The MTV mindset and the rest of our media saturated culture aren't waiting to spread their messages about sex to your child. Ultimately, you have to decide who will get there first.

PULLING BACK THE CURTAINS

"The Talk" has become the most awkward and memorable moment of adolescence for much of the adult population. Why are we so tied to having one of the most difficult conversations imposed on the stage of development most people want to forget? Do you remember the kids in your middle school classes? It's not likely. The memory of your parents having "The Talk" with you, however, is probably clearer than the headlines in yesterday's news.

I have several problems with "The Talk." As I just stated, the early

character in 60 minutes! I think it's also appropriate to recognize that kids at this stage are "bio-chemically challenged"—the ebb and flow of their hormones creates an environment of unpredictability; a temporary insanity, if you will. Those who have already guided a child through this stage of life know exactly what I'm talking about.

teen years are a developmentally difficult phase for most people, and they seem predisposed to question authority. At this time of life, children do not view their parents as the wise authority. They are naturally beginning to build walls and look to others to process and evaluate the world they are excited to explore. In addition, talking about sex should take place over a number of years, not minutes. You cannot effectively shape your child's sexual

Unlike teenagers, 4-, 5- and 6-year-olds generally don't torture their parents just because they can! In their minds, Mommy and Daddy are those nice people they cling to who know everything about everything and would never lie to them.

So how do I answer the question, "How did that baby get in there?

Start by going back to step one. Go back to your overarching message. (This is one of the reasons it is so important to love your big picture message.) Using the space on page 89, craft a couple of sentences to explain conception based on those core beliefs and values you already established in your household.

Use accurate information and stick to the facts. We're just talking about basic biology. There's nothing sensual about this stage of discussion. For the sake of clarification, I'll share what the sentences Dave and I crafted under the Ridley banner message that "Sex is a gift from God for marriage." When asked, "How did that baby get in there?", we had already developed our response: **"Well, I am so glad you asked. You know what, sweetheart? By God's design a husband and a wife were made to fit together in a very special way. And when that happens part of what is deep inside of Daddy meets with of part of what is deep inside of Mommy and that is what God uses to start the baby."**

That was it. I hope you are not too disappointed. All we needed was a first impression. We knew that this would not be our last conversation with our child, so we didn't want or need to cover everything at once. Developmentally speaking, it would be too much for them to process, anyway. The simple goal at this point is to pick up their little feet and point them in the direction you want them to go. You want to include your values, your beliefs and the basic biology—all without giving them a lot of detail they really don't need at this point. A gauzy picture is perfectly adequate and appropriate at the beginning.

This is the opposite of "The Talk." It's presenting different levels of information at different stages of their lives, making each conversation a building block for the next one. Another way to think of it is like painting a beautiful piece of art. You don't sit down, plaster the canvas with tons of paint and complete it all in one setting. A masterpiece takes time. You have 10 to 15 years to paint a complete picture of sex, with all of its mysteries, wonders, dangers, pleasures, details and complications coming in the

If our children ever asked us anything about sex, Dave and I had a policy to smile and say, "I am so glad you asked." We wanted them to know we were so pleased that they came to us with their question. An additional benefit of this policy was that it served as a handy stall tactic, giving us a few extra moments to formulate what we were going to say next.

later stages of development. Having "the talk" isn't pretty or skillful—or very effective. Start with some thin curtains in front of the completed work of art, and pull back a curtain as it becomes appropriate for their stage of development.

If your child is outgoing and potentially the smartest kid on the block, chances are that revealing the first curtain alone is not going to satisfy his or her curiosity. If that's not enough, the logical next question they'll want answered is, "What do you mean 'fits together' in a very special way?"

You can tackle that one by giving more detail, but keeping it within the overall banner statement

you developed. Our response was something like this: "Well, honey, it is really pretty amazing. Here's what happens. By God's design the husband places his penis inside of the wife's vagina. (You can say that part faster if you want to, but be sure to use those proper terms.) The part that is deep inside the Daddy is called the sperm and it travels through the penis and meets with the egg that is deep inside the Mommy. That is how they fit together. It was designed for oneness in marriage and also for making babies."

In truth, this is not as difficult as it sounds, but I encourage you to practice saying it, because saying it while looking into their sweet little faces may affect your ability to find the words on the fly. Keep in mind that talking about sex doesn't have to be as daunting as you think because at these stages you don't have to bring all of the dangers and emotional complexities into the conversation. Limit it to basic biology wrapped in your family values.

YOUR CHILD'S RESPONSE

Don't be surprised if your child has an unexpected reaction to your explanation of intercourse. After discussing it with one of my children, her reaction was, "That's so gross!" It's important not to respond negatively to that expression of feeling. Instead, seek to assure your child that you completely

understand how they could feel that way at their age. It's much like when they were a baby. In the early stages of development, their hunger was satisfied with milk. A cheeseburger would not have been appropriate, nor appealing. As they grew, however, a juicy burger became very appealing. It's part of the changes that take place as they grow and mature. You can ask them to simply trust you that, in time, they will feel differently about the design of sex.

MAKE IT YOURS!

STEP 6:

LAUNCH TOWARD ADOLESCENCE

 TRANSITIONING TO PUBERTY

The next critical stage of developing your child's sexual character is preparing them for what's coming as the onset of puberty approaches. It's very important that you not get to this conversation late. About a year before the onset of adolescence, plan a special get away with your child. Perhaps you can take them camping over the weekend, or borrow a friend's lake house, or go on a nature excursion, or drive to the country and stay at a bed and breakfast.

The point is to get away from the familiar and the distractions of their routine lives in order to carve out a time conducive to focusing on the communication you are about to have. It's time to take the conversation to a new level; one that now includes the introduction of the dangers and pleasures associated with sexuality. You will need to discuss how their body is about to change so it doesn't shock or embarrass them. You want to take the guesswork out of the ways they're going to mature physically, intellectually, emotionally, socially and spiritually. You also want to prepare them for how your relationship may change in the coming years.

As I've mentioned before, you should seek to have these important conversations with your child, BEFORE they stop listening to you and start listening to other, less

credible sources. If you wait until they're 16, you will have missed your opportunity by years, not months.

In a perfect world, I recommend moms take their daughters and fathers take their sons. Prior to this stage, it's less important who is doing the talking. When it comes to the physical changes of puberty, your child is more likely to feel comfortable talking with a parent of the same sex. I know that's not the dangers, pleasures, risks and rewards associated with adolescent sexual health. Children are naturally

Sometimes children ask about our past and parents struggle with their decision of how much to share. This challenge should be met by answering the question: "What would be the most helpful to my child?" Sometimes a simple answer, such as, "I have some regrets that I don't want you to have," will suffice. Sometimes more information is required.

always possible, especially for single parents, but single parents can easily arm themselves with good books and advise from trusted friends before they enter into these conversations. Regardless of who the messenger is, the most important thing is to now introduce them to

curious. When they're at the age of being capable and interested in being sexually active, you do not want them to searching for answers at the school of hard knocks. If experience is the greatest teacher of all, then use yours to educate your children.

PRESENTING A TIMELINE

One of my favorite tools parents can use during this special time away is a life timeline (see illustration). Using a couple sheets of paper taped end to end, draw a line across the center and the back of the line 88. Ask your child to talk about their life so far up to age 10, 11 or 12. Ask them to name the highlights of their life so far. Make notches in the timeline to represent the years of their life, and write out the highlights of the past at

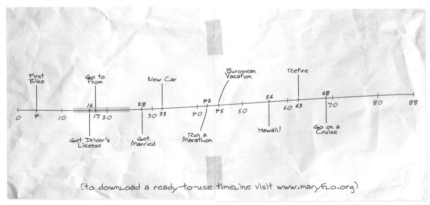

(to download a ready-to-use timeline visit www.maryflo.org)

that spans the length of the pages. Label the front of the line age 0

the appropriate place they occurred on the timeline.

Now shift the conversation to the future highlights they hope to achieve. These may include milestones like graduating from high school, earning a college degree, starting a career, getting married, traveling to other countries, having children, becoming a grandparent, retiring, etc. Ask your child questions like: "What are your dreams?" and "How long do you expect it to take to accomplish each of them?" Have your child pencil in on the timeline approximate dates they hope to reach those goals. Once completed, point out how the teen years are a very small portion of the timeline. With that in mind, emphasize to them that the decisions they make in that short window of time, in particular with respect to drugs,

alcohol, tobacco, unmarried sex and pornography, can have a permanent effect on the rest of their lives. Be very direct and clear with them that you love them and want the best for them, so they need to understand this: If they can steer clear of those five destructive behaviors, they will significantly increase their chances of achieving their future dreams. If they don't, they are putting the goals and dreams on their timeline at risk. Remind them that you truly believe they can, and that it's your passionate hope that they will.

Before you head out for the weekend, spend plenty of time preparing for what you want to say. You may need to do some research to become better informed on how to cover the toughest aspects of sexual activity. This is the time to directly discuss challenging questions like, "What is oral sex?", "What is masturbation", "How do you feel about contraception?" and "How would you react if I told you I was pregnant?"

While all of these topics can be difficult to discuss, they are not nearly as tough as the potential ramifications of the unhealthy choices your child may make without accurate and personal information provided by you on these controversial issues.

Although this will not be an easy weekend, I firmly believe it can be one of the meaningful and rewarding things you can do for your relationship with your child and their future healthy and safety.

SEIZING THE OPPORTUNITY

It's important to launch them in this manner so that you can grant them a positive and supportive take off on their flight toward adulthood. Launch your child well and you'll be far more likely to be able to enjoy their high school days, rather then constantly worrying about the mistakes you fear they're going to make. I'm already on the other side of those days and I assure you that you'll still worry about them, but the day they move out is constantly drawing nearer and you don't want to miss enjoying the time you still have with them.

Those days may seem like light years away, but you won't believe how quickly they come. I challenge and encourage you to engage your child now and pass along the information and skills they need to pursue and attain healthy relationships.

At this stage of your child's growth, discussions about the dangers and pleasures of sex are the tough task at hand. If you have invested time over the years discussing tough issues and cultivating trust with your child, these conversations can be extremely encouraging and rewarding. Do the job early and well and your child will be ready to listen and take your counsel to heart.

The truth is, there are no guarantees that your child will embrace your vision and direction for their sexual character. Regardless of their behavior, however, make the commitment to never give up talking. When a difficult situation arises, they need to know you are still there for them. And you need to know that you did everything you could to help them achieve their dreams.

MAKE IT YOURS!

▸ Are you prepared to talk with your child about the lasting impact of sexually transmitted diseases? Nonmarital pregnancy? Dating violence?

▸ Are you comfortable talking with your kids about how drugs and alcohol can influence their decisions, and how the ramifications can be life changing?

Toolkit

While I cannot prepare you for all of the discussions you need to have with your child during this important weekend, I can recommend several resources. The first is a book I mentioned earlier, *Questions Kids Ask About Sex*. This helpful tool has straightforward answers to the questions your child will have about relationships and sexual intimacy.

For help in discussing issues like STDs/STIs, alcohol, drugs, pornography, dating violence, eating disorders, brain development and more, my friends at Just Say YES have developed a creative video/discussion guide series called "Look Before You Leap: Class Packs" that is a fun, powerful tool for stimulating great conversations and passing on information that can make a difference in your child's life.

To order these and other great resources for parents and teens call (888) 579-5790 or visit www.JustSayYES.org.

MAKE IT YOURS!

CON CLU SION

I recently heard a story that stuck in my head. On a popular TV talk show, a mother, her 10-year-old daughter, a doctor and the host were conversing. The subject of the program was that this 10-year-old wanted her mother to talk to her about sex, but her mother was paralyzed with fear. It was easy to see why she was so overwhelmed: She had waited, and now, in her mind, the subject was too large for her to handle.

This mom had missed the opportunity to discuss what her daughter needed to know along the way, and now it had become too awkward and overwhelming to initiate.

My heart went out to her, and I wished I could turn back the clock for her. Her daughter was not given the opportunity to enjoy the mysteries and magic of having these progressive conversations as she grew. They were on national TV not only discussing basic biology, but also sex toys and many other things that weren't age-appropriate for a 10-year-old—especially one that has no foundation to build upon. The doctor and host treated this like it was the

only opportunity this girl would ever have to learn about sex. They dumped the entire bucket on her sponge. Since her sponge was completely dry, she absorbed what they poured into her (rather than the healthy messages her mother could have drip-dripped into her daughter's mind). It was tragic. Fortunately your child doesn't ever have to be in that situation.

I hope this presentation has encouraged you and prepared you for the privilege that's before you of shaping your child's sexual character. As a mother of three grown children, I can tell you I don't regret for a second what Dave and I have shared with our children. Even though we didn't do it perfectly, I believe their lives are significantly better as a result of us passing on age-appropriate information about sex as they grew up in a manner that was respectful to their innocence and curiosity.

My utmost hope for you is that at least one essential "Simple Truth" sinks in as a result of your time spent with this presentation: Shaping your child's sexual character is one of the greatest privileges of parenting.

The time is now to embrace it and give your child the best possible chance at achieving their goals and dreams for the future. It's a legacy you can leave that not only affects the child you love, but also the future spouse they will become.

Let the journey begin!

> **Viewer's Note:** The "Simple Truths Step-by-Step" DVD concludes with two Additional Insights video clips which address "Cultural and Media Influences" and "Modesty and Privacy." These broad topics are important, but don't uniquely apply to any one of the specified steps presented on this DVD.

About the Author

In 1986, Mary Flo Ridley began presenting a popular parenting seminar in the Dallas area. The original title was "Guiding Your Children's Sexual Values." At that time she and her husband, Dave, had two children ages four and one. They have now been married for 30 years and their children have grown up and left the nest.

After growing up in El Paso, Texas, Mary Flo graduated from Southern Methodist University in Dallas, and taught high school for four years. In a volunteer capacity she was a trainer for a community service organization, where she developed several training programs for members.

In addition to her national speaking engagements, Mary Flo is actively involved in her church and community, and loves being a wife, mother and friend.

About the Publisher

Just Say YES was established to provide youth with factual and relational information equipping them to live healthy and successful lives. Working with individuals, educators, community officials and policymakers, Just Say YES offers communities a wide array of resources to positively impact the lives and futures of their young people.

SPECIAL THANKS

"I want to express my love and thanks to my precious husband, Dave, for his constant prayers and encouragement, and to our amazing children for their love and support. We are so proud of you!

With great thanks to everyone at Just Say YES, especially to Dan, for asking me to be part of the team. This could not have happened without you all! Patrick and The Table Group for your affirming help at a critical time...thank you. Thank you, Alan and Melissa for using your gifts to make my dream a reality. I thank God for the gift of this message."

Mary Flo Ridley
National Speaker
www.MaryFloBlog.com

To Mary Flo, thank you for the care and devotion to parents of young children that made this project possible. Your encouraging, entertaining, life-changing program sparked a need to multiply your message. Thank you for allowing us to take your live program to homes throughout the nation! Thank you to Cox Creative (Alan and Melissa), your creative collaboration, commitment to excellence and dedication to positively impacting parents have transformed a concept into a powerful real-life product. To our generous donors and the Council for Life, without your financial generosity, this dream would still be on the whiteboard! To the amazing Just Say YES staff whose collective work and feedback helped make "Simple Truths" materialize, you are awesome! And finally, to all of the parents, PTA/PTOs, MOPS groups, parent groups and churches that have sent encouraging feedback and ideas after hearing Mary Flo's live program—"Sooner Than You Think"—thank you for embracing this critical message.

Dan Bailey
Executive Director, **Just Say YES**

Youth Equipped to Succeed

PO Box 670863, Dallas, TX 75367
972 437 0002
Toll Free: 888 579 5790
Email: info@justsayyes.org
www.JustSayYES.org

Just Say YES was established to provide youth with factual and relational information that equips them to live healthy, successful lives. Working with individuals, educators, community officials and policymakers, **Just Say YES** offers communities a wide array of resources to positively impact the lives and futures of young people.

Questions Kids Ask About Sex

This easy to read, comprehensive guide helps educators, parents and others working with youth get prepared and comfortable with discussing the key questions young people ask about sex.

NOTES

Get or Give The Complete Set!

This discussion guide is just one part of the **Simple Truths with Mary Flo Ridley Complete Set**, which features a DVD and audio CD of Mary Flo's live presentation, "Sooner Than You Think," as well as a Step-By-Step DVD presentation that explores each of the sections in far greater depth and detail.

To purchase, visit www.MaryFlo.org or call Just Say YES at 1-888-579-5790 or email info@justsayyes.org.

TO ORDER OR LEARN MORE CALL (972) 437-0002